THE LETTER BOOK

MEKO

Copyright © 2020 Meko
All rights reserved.

ISBN: 978-0-578-65747-9
Library of Congress Control
Number: 2020905052
Eagle Life
Publications, Dallas, TX

AIRPLANE

ANT

ANIMALS

ASTRONAUT

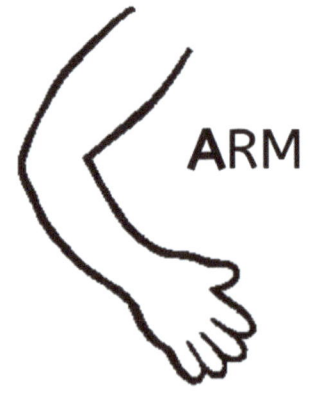  

ARM   **A**X   **A**PPLE

 **B** is for...

BIRD

 **B**US

BIKE

 **B**EE

 **B**ABY

BANANA

BALL

 is for...
CAR

CRAB
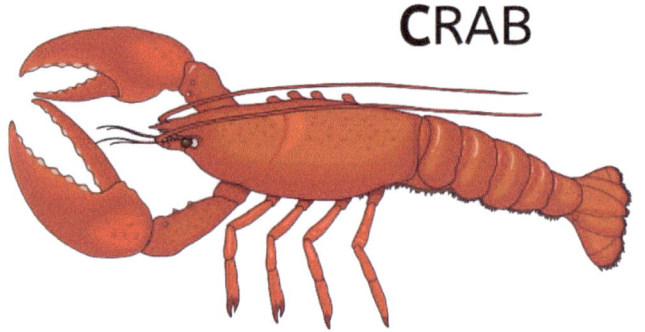

CUPCAKE

COUCH

CUP
COW

CORN

 is for...

DEER

DESK

DRUM

DUCK

DOOR

DRESS

 is for...

ELEPHANT

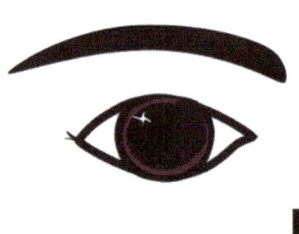

EYES

EIGHT

EAGLE

EGGS

EARTH

 is for... **F**IRE TRUCK

FLOWERS

FISH

FIRE

FRUIT

FOOTBALL

FROG

 is for...

ICICLES

IGLOO

INSECTS

ICE

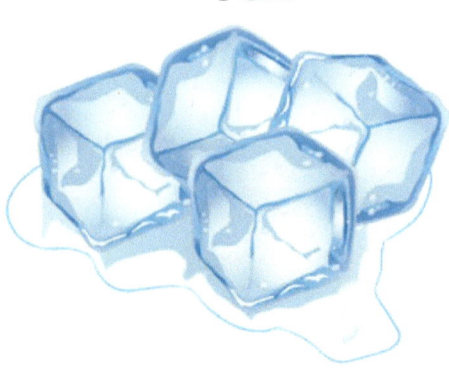

ICE CREAM

ISLAND

 is for...

LION

LEAVES

LADDER

LADYBUG

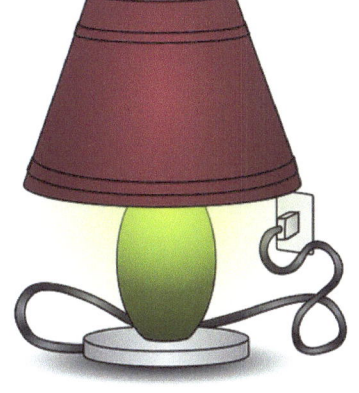
LAMP

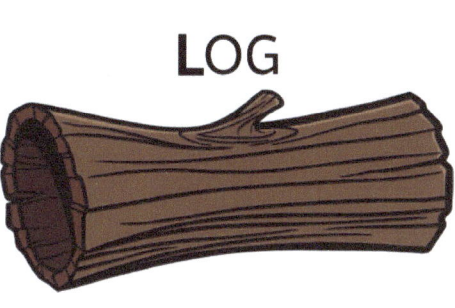
LOG

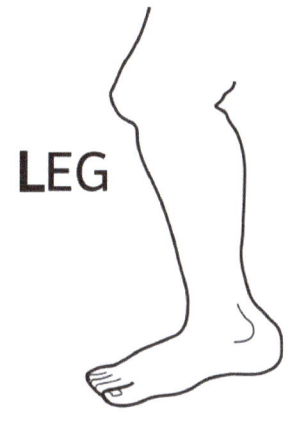
LEG

 is for...

NURSE

 **N**EST

 **N**OODLES

NUMBERS  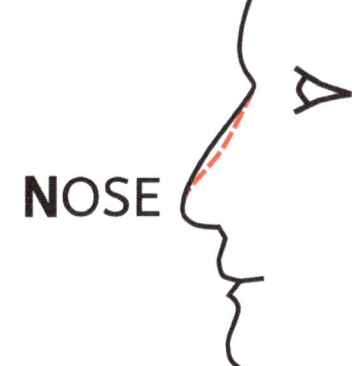 **N**OSE

 **N**UTS

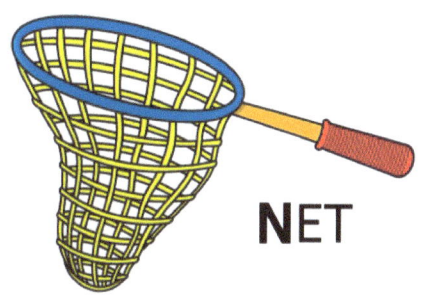 **N**ET

 is for...

OX

OWL

OSTRICH

ORANGES

OCTOPUS

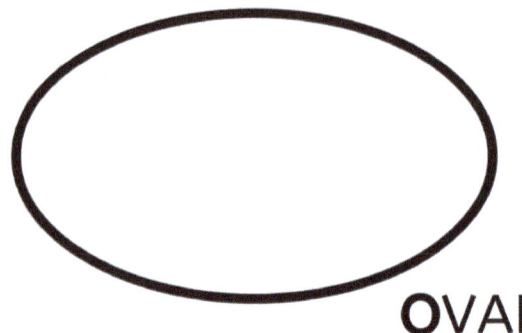

OVAL

 is for...

PLANTS

PINEAPPLES **P**UMPKIN

POT

PIE **P**OLICE

PENCIL

 is for...   **R**HINO

RABBIT

RAIN

ROBOT

ROCKET

RACCOON   **R**ING

 is for...

SAD

 **S**KATES

 **S**NOWMAN

 **S**HOES

 **S**TRAWBERRY

 **S**NAKE

 **S**TAR

 **S**UN

 is for... **T**UB

TRUCK

TURTLE

TIGER

TENT

TREE

THREE

 is for... **U**NICORN

UNIFORMS

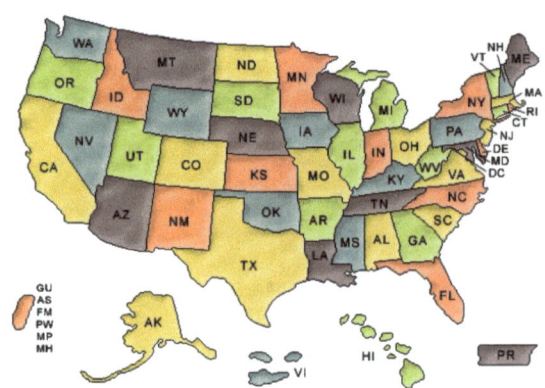 **U**SA

UMBRELLA

UTENSILS

UNICYCLE

UP

 is for... **V**EGETABLES

VAN

VIOLIN

VASE

VOLCANO

VEST

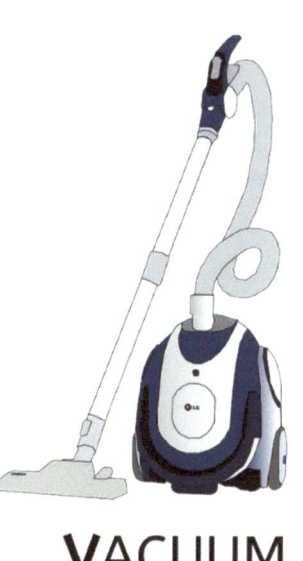
VACUUM

W is for...

WAGON

WATERMELON

WHEEL

WATCH

WHISTLE

WATER

WHALE

 **Y** is for...

YACHT

YAK

YARN

YOLK
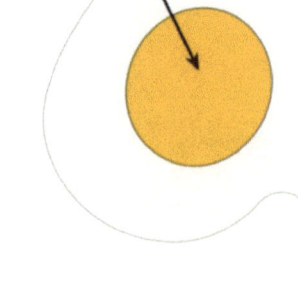

YAWN

YOGURT

 **Y**O-YO

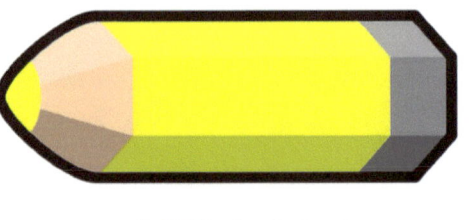
YELLOW

 is for...
ZERO

ZEBRA

ZUCCHINI

ZOO

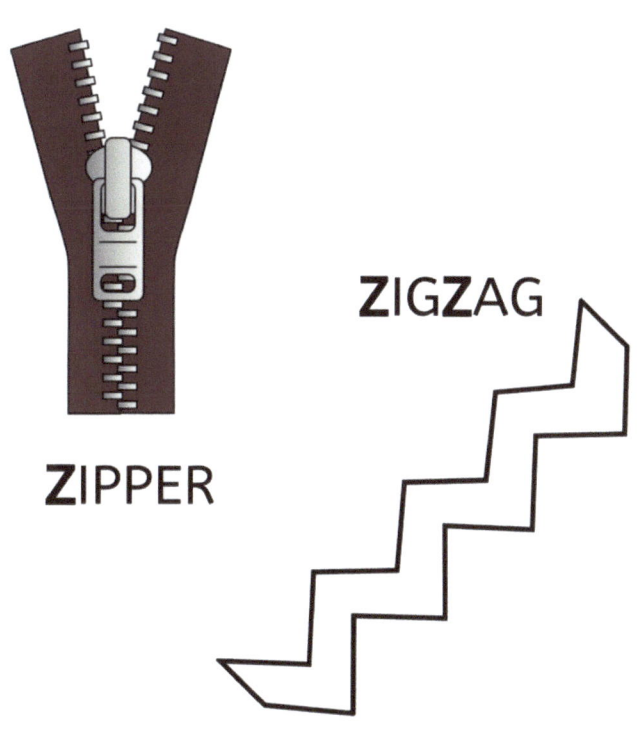
ZIPPER **Z**IG**Z**AG

DOLPHINS

SMART & EARLY LEARNING

CROWN

GIFT

For more information about Meko's Smart & Early Learning initiative, visit www.eaglelifepublications.net

WORM

CHEESE

HORN

www.ingramcontent.com/pod-product-compliance
Lightning Source LLC
Chambersburg PA
CBHW041229040426
42444CB00002B/108